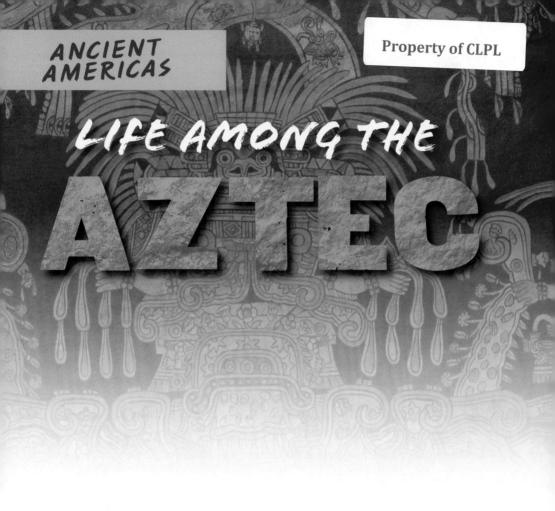

LIFE AMONG THE
AZTEC

RACHEL STUCKEY

PowerKiDS
press.

NEW YORK

Published in 2017 by **The Rosen Publishing Group, Inc.**
29 East 21st Street, New York, NY 10010

Developed and produced for Rosen by BlueAppleWorks Inc.

Art Director: Haley Harasymiw
Managing Editor for BlueAppleWorks: Melissa McClellan
Editor: Marcia Abramson
Design: T.J. Choleva

Picture credits: Cover: frgrd. f9photos/Shutterstock; bkgrd. Jiri Vaclavek/Shutterstock. Back cover: frgrd.
Artishok/Shutterstock; bkgrd. altanaka/Shutterstock. Title page Thomas Aleto/Creative Commons; p. 5 José
María Jara/Public Domain; p. 9 El Comandante(mural Diego Rivera)/Creative Commons; p. 10 Diego Rivera/
Public Domain; p. 13 Hans Hillewaert/CC-BY-SA-4.0; p. 14 Public Domain; p. 17 Mike Peel (www.mikepeel.
net)/ CC-BY-SA-4.0; p. 19 JHMimaging/Shutterstock; p. 19 left Dennis Jarvis/Creative Commons; p. 19 right
Simon Burchell/Creative Commons; p. 20 inset Marcelo Rodriguez/Shutterstock; p. 20 Anna Omelchenko/
Shutterstock; p. 21 Jonathan Cardy/Creative Commons; p. 21 inset Martin M303/Shutterstock; p. 22
Public Domain; p. 23 left sailko/Creative Commons; p. 23 top GFDL CC-BY-SA; p. 23 Thomas Ledl/Creative
Commons; p. 23 bottom right Ondrej Prosicky/Shutterstock; p. 24 jejim/Shutterstock; p. 24 right Luidger/
Creative Commons; p. 25, 25 left Vadim Petrakov/Shutterstock; p. 25 right Leon Rafael/Shutterstock; p.
27 Antonio Rodriguez/Public Domain; p. 29, 29 inset, posztos/Shutterstock; Maps: p. 5 inset T.J. Choleva/
Sémhu/Creative Commons; p. 6 T.J. Choleva IndianSummer/Shutterstock

Cataloging-in-Publication Data

Names: Stuckey, Rachel.
Title: Life among the Aztec / Rachel Stuckey.
Description: New York : PowerKids Press, 2017. | Series: Ancient Americas | Includes index.
Identifiers: ISBN 9781508149859 (pbk.) | ISBN 9781508149798 (library bound) | ISBN 9781508149675 (6 pack)
Subjects: LCSH: Aztecs--Juvenile literature. | Indians of Mexico--Juvenile literature.
Classification: LCC F1219.73 S78 2017| DDC 972'.00497452--dc23

Manufactured in the United States of America

CPSIA Compliance Information: Batch #BS16PK: For Further Information contact Rosen Publishing, New York, New York at 1-800-237-9932

CONTENTS

CHAPTER 1

LEGEND OF THE AZTECS

The great Aztec Empire ruled central Mexico for 100 years. The Aztec peoples recorded their history, wrote poetry, studied astronomy, and amazed the Spanish **conquistadors** with their great cities and towering pyramid temples. The Aztecs are actually a group of tribes who spoke the Nahuatl language. These tribes started to arrive in the Valley of Mexico around A.D. 600. Over time they became farmers and their settlements grew into cities. Historians believe the Nahua peoples came from somewhere in northern Mexico or even the American Southwest.

Around 1250, a new tribe called the Mexica arrived on the shores of Lake Texcoco. According to Aztec legend, the Mexica came from a **mythical** country called Aztlan. The Mexica also spoke Nahua, but they seemed uncivilized compared to the Toltec, Tepanec, Acolhua, and Xochimilca peoples who had settled there hundreds of years earlier. These cultures lived in complex city-states, but the Mexica were still **nomadic** hunters. But in 1323, the Mexica received a sign from their god, Huitzilopochtli, and built their own city called Tenochtitlán. The wealth and power of Tenochtitlán quickly grew. In 1427, the Mexica allied with two other Nahua cities and founded an **alliance** that we now call the Aztec Empire.

Azcapotzalco

Texcoco

Lake
Texcoco

Tenochtitlán

Tlacopan

Culhuacan

AN ANCIENT PROPHECY LED
THE MEXICA TO A MUDDY
ISLAND IN LAKE TEXCOCO.

5

THE EMPIRE

The Nahua city-states around Lake Texcoco were in a constant struggle for power and control. Soon after the Mexica arrived, the Tepanecs of Azcapotzalco expelled them from their territory. The Toltecs of Culhuacan then gave the Mexica a place to settle on the southern shores of Lake Texcoco. The Mexica built their own city on an island in the lake. For their own protection, the Mexica of Tenochtitlán had to pay tribute to the powerful Tepanecs of Azcapotzalco—a city on the western shores of Lake Texcoco.

But the Mexica grew more and more powerful and wealthy. Eventually the city of Tenochtitlán allied with the Acolhua of Texcoco, a city on the eastern shore of the lake, and the Tepanecs of Tlacopan, a city next to Azcapotzalco. Together these cities formed the Aztec Triple Alliance. The alliance defeated the city of Azcapotzalco and went on to conquer many other cities. Each conquered city was

Aztec Triple Alliance territories (1428 – 1521)

North America

Atlantic Ocean

Gulf of Mexico

Pacific Ocean

South America

Mexico

Tenochtitlán

Yucatán Peninsula

Pacific Ocean

required to pay tribute to the alliance, just like the Mexica had paid tribute to Azcapotzalco. The alliance, led by the Mexica, became what we now call the Aztec Empire.

SPANISH CONQUEST

The Aztec Empire reached its height at the end of the 1400s. Tenochtitlán was the largest city in the Americas, and the empire controlled territory from the Pacific Ocean to the Gulf of Mexico. But everything changed when explorers from Spain arrived in the Caribbean in 1492. A Spanish **expedition** lead by Hernán Cortés landed in Maya territory on the Gulf Coast in 1519, and arrived in Tenochtitlán in the summer of 1520. At first they were welcomed but after some conflict with the Aztecs, the Spanish fled. But in the spring of 1521 Cortés returned with a larger army that laid **siege** to the city. By August the Spanish had defeated the city and controlled the empire. Later the Spanish would build their own capital, Mexico City, on top of the ruins of Tenochtitlán. From there they ran their colonization of Central America.

What's in the name?

The Aztecs did not call themselves "the Aztecs." "Aztec" actually means "people from Aztlan." There were many Mesoamerican cultures in and around the empire that believed they came from the same mythical Aztlan. At the time, almost everyone was considered to be Aztec!

CHAPTER 2

TENOCHTITLÁN

Tenochtitlán was the city of the gods. The Mexica had no home in the Valley of Mexico. But legend says that in 1323, the Aztec god Huitzilopochtli led them to an island in Lake Texcoco, where they had a vision. There they saw an eagle perched on a prickly pear cactus with a snake in its beak. The Mexica believed this was a sign from Huitzilopochtli. The island was muddy and swampy, but the Mexica built it up with more mud and connected it to other, smaller islands nearby. In 1325 they began to build their city. In 1375, they elected their first king or tlatoani. The word "tlatoani" actually means "speaker."

The first building was a temple to honor Huitzilopochtli and the god of rain, Tlaloc. What the Spanish called the Templo Mayor was a huge pyramid with stairways leading to the **shrines** at the top.

Mexican flag and Aztec legend

At the center of the modern Mexican flag there is an eagle with a snake in its beak and the eagle is perched on a cactus. The flag represents Mexico's Aztec history and the founding of the city of Tenochtitlán.

TENOCHTITLÁN WAS ONE OF THE GREATEST CITIES IN MESOAMERICA WITH OVER 200,000 RESIDENTS.

9

SPANISH EXPLORERS COUNTED 78 BUILDINGS IN THE SACRED PRECINCT. THEY NAMED THE TALLEST ONE (LEFT) TEMPLO MAYOR, WHICH MEANS "GREAT TEMPLE."

The Mexica kept a fire burning day and night at the top of each shrine. Around the temple was the sacred precinct with public buildings, smaller temples, and the emperor's palace of 100 rooms.

The city around the sacred precinct was built according to a plan. The island city was linked to the shores of the lake by three bridge-like causeways going north, south, and west. There were canals throughout the city and all the streets ran north–south or east–west. Because the lake water was muddy, the Mexica built **aqueducts** to bring fresh water to the city from miles away. At the height of the Aztec Empire, Tenochtitlán was the largest city in the Americas and probably one of the largest cities in the world.

LIFE IN TENOCHTITLÁN

Tenochtitlán was a crowded city, but healthy—thanks to the freshwater aqueducts. The canals were lined with willow trees and small gardens. Streets were narrow because they were designed for walking. There were no large animals or wheeled vehicles in Mesoamerica, so goods were transported by porters on foot or small boats and canoes.

The city was also well organized—divided into four sections called campans. Each campan was divided into smaller neighborhoods called calpolli, or "big houses." Each calpolli included families from all social classes that lived together as a small community within the city. People visited the market every day. As there was no money, people bartered for goods. Cacao beans, blankets, shells, feathers, gold, and silver were all used in trade.

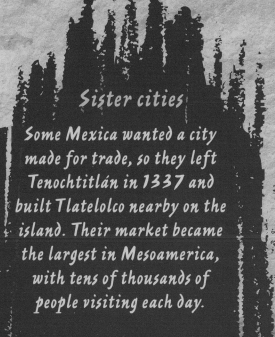

Tenochtitlán had very little land, but the Aztecs had learned to farm in the shallow shores of the lake. They raised the land using mud and grasses to create artificial islands called chinampas. The farmers would travel between these fertile farming beds by canoe.

Sister cities

Some Mexica wanted a city made for trade, so they left Tenochtitlán in 1337 and built Tlatelolco nearby on the island. Their market became the largest in Mesoamerica, with tens of thousands of people visiting each day.

CHAPTER 3

AZTEC EMPIRE

Having a strong military was important to the peoples of Mesoamerica. The city-states were always going to war with each other. The losing city would have to pay tributes or make payments to the winning city, in return for its continuing safety. For many years Tenochtitlán was a tribute city to Azcapotzalco, a city of the Tepanec. But in the 1420s a war broke out between several Tepanec cities and instead of supporting Azcapotzalco, the Mexica of Tenochtitlán turned against the city. Tenochtitlán joined with the Tepanec city of Tlacopan and the Acolhua city of Texcoco and formed the Aztec Triple Alliance.

The Triple Alliance won the civil war and divided the Tepanec cities and lands between them. Winning the war did not bring a time of peace. To maintain their power and dominance, the alliance had to keep conquering cities. The alliance relied on the tributes the cities paid. The people of the alliance also needed a source of captives to use for **human sacrifice**—an important part of the Aztec religion. Taking captives was the goal of every Aztec warrior.

Over the next 100 years, what we now call the Aztec Empire stretched from the Gulf of Mexico to the Pacific Ocean and as far south as modern-day Guatemala.

TEZCATLIPOCA WAS THE SPECIAL GOD OF KINGS AND WARRIORS. THIS MOSAIC MASK OF THE FIERCE GOD WAS CREATED FROM A SKULL.

13

AS SOLDIERS MOVED UP IN RANK, THEIR CLOTHES, JEWELRY, AND HAIRSTYLES BECAME MORE SPECTACULAR.

THE AZTEC ARMY

The Aztec Empire relied on its army, so being a warrior was the most important job in Aztec society. All boys had military training. A soldier's rank in the army was based on his success on the battlefield. The nobility were all members of warrior societies. Each society had a different style of dress and jewelry. One warrior society was the Papalotl, or "Butterflies." These men had taken three captives and wore butterfly banners on their backs. The only way a commoner could improve his social status was by winning battles and taking captives. Commoners who impressed the nobility on the battlefield joined special warrior societies such as the Eagles or the Jaguars.

AZTEC TRADERS

Trade was very important to the empire. The Aztecs traded goods between cities and brought back goods from faraway places. The Aztecs did not have wagons or horses so traders used canoes and slaves to transport goods. Merchants or traders were well respected in Aztec society, but they held a strange place in the class structure. They were very wealthy, but because they were considered commoners, they were not supposed to display their wealth in public.

THE AZTEC SOCIETY

Each calpolli, or "big house," in the city was made up of families that were related to each other in some way. Sometimes it was family relationships or type of work. Almost everything Aztec people did happened within their calpolli. However, Aztec society was also strictly divided into nobles, called pipiltin, and commoners, called macehualli. The nobles led their calpolli and owned the land. The commoners worked for the nobles and farmed their land.

There were many divisions within each class and many rules about how each class could dress. Commoners who earned higher status through battle were treated like nobles but still considered commoners because Aztec class divisions were very strict. Merchants were also a separate class—they were considered commoners but had special status because of their wealth.

The Aztecs also had slaves to provide labor. Captives taken in battle often became slaves. People who committed crimes were often punished by becoming slaves. Also, people who owed money could pay off their debts by becoming temporary slaves.

CHAPTER 4

LIFE IN THE AZTEC EMPIRE

Aztecs waged constant wars to keep their empire strong and to assure a steady supply of captives for religious ceremonies. Therefore, the entire Aztec culture revolved around building and maintaining an army of warriors.

Some traders also worked as spies for the military, bringing back intelligence about faraway cities that they visited. In return, Aztec warriors often joined trading expeditions to dangerous places to protect the merchants and their goods.

FAMILY LIFE

The most important role for Aztec men was that of soldier. At birth, Aztec boys were given a shield and an arrow made specifically for them. Then, a great warrior would take these items and bury them on a battlefield with the boy's **umbilical cord**.

Almost all Aztec men had to serve in the military. When boys went to school to begin their military training, they started to grow a lock of hair. This lock would not be cut off until the boy had captured a prisoner in battle. Capturing prisoners was the most important task for Aztec warriors. Killing enemy soldiers in the battlefield was considered crude and clumsy.

THIS ALMOST LIFE-SIZE STATUE OF AN EAGLE WARRIOR WAS FOUND IN TENOCHTITLÁN. EAGLES AND JAGUARS WERE THE MOST FEARED AND RESPECTED AZTEC MILITARY ORDERS.

17

After serving in the military, men would take on the profession of their father. They were farmers, craftsmen, or merchants. Those commoners who did well in battle often held a higher status and might be able to send their sons to religious schools.

Women's place in Aztec society was taking care of the home—they were not allowed in the military. They spun cloth, tended animals, and prepared food. Aztec women had to spend much of their day grinding corn to make flour. Their domestic role was very important—when a baby girl was born, her umbilical cord was buried beneath the fireplace to symbolize her importance in the home. But early Aztec women had some equality with men. Women did take on jobs as professional weavers and crafters, and some were even priests and doctors.

Women who died in childbirth were treated just like warriors who died in battle. It was believed they would rise to the Sun God instead of going to the underworld.

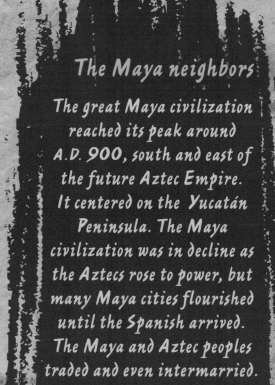

The Maya neighbors

The great Maya civilization reached its peak around A.D. 900, south and east of the future Aztec Empire. It centered on the Yucatán Peninsula. The Maya civilization was in decline as the Aztecs rose to power, but many Maya cities flourished until the Spanish arrived. The Maya and Aztec peoples traded and even intermarried.

USING A CEREMONIAL KNIFE, AZTEC PRIESTS MADE HUMAN SACRIFICES TO IMPORTANT GODS SUCH AS QUETZALCOATL (LEFT).

RELIGION AND WORSHIP

The Aztecs worshipped Huitzilopochtli, the god of the sun and war. Huitzilopochtli became the central focus of Aztec worship when the Mexica built Tenochtitlán. Other **deities** included Tonatiuh (sun god), Tlaloc (god of rain), and Quetzalcoatl (feathered serpent), among others. Aztec temples were built at the top of pyramids.

In Aztec mythology, the deities sacrificed themselves to create human life. To honor that, the Aztecs practiced human sacrifice. Human sacrifice was common in Mesoamerica and it is believed that the people considered it an honor to be sacrificed. The Aztec Empire needed captives so that they could keep the gods happy with their sacrifice. One historical record says the Aztecs sacrificed thousands of prisoners in one four-day ceremony.

ARCHITECTURE

The Aztecs are most well known for their pyramids. Aztec pyramids were temples meant to look like mountains. Unlike Egyptian pyramids, Aztec pyramids had steps up to a flat top. The Aztecs built these great stone structures from limestone that they were able to **quarry** without any metal tools.

The Aztecs often built larger pyramids and temples over the original. The Templo Mayor was first built in 1325 and rebuilt six or seven times. The last version of it was destroyed by the Spanish in the 1520s, but **archaeologists** have found older versions underneath modern-day Mexico City. Aztecs built very grand palaces. Moctezuma's palace in Tenochtitlán had 100 rooms, each with its own bath.

THE STEEP PYRAMIDS OF TEOTIHUACAN, AN ANCIENT RUIN 30 MILES (48 KM) FROM TENOCHTITLÁN, INSPIRED THE AZTEC BUILDING STYLE. TO THIS DAY, LITTLE IS KNOWN ABOUT THE PEOPLE OF THE RUINED CITY.

JUST AS THE AZTECS DID, PEOPLE TODAY MAKE TRIPS TO VISIT TEOTIHUACAN. THE AZTEC NAME MEANS "THE PLACE WHERE THE GODS WERE CREATED."

Outside the sacred precinct, most people lived in houses made of wood, reeds, and mud plaster with thatch roofs. Wealthier commoners had houses built from **adobe** bricks. The nobility had houses made of stone. All buildings had to be approved by the city's planners, no matter how small. This helped keep the city symmetrical and ordered—one of the reasons the Spanish were so impressed.

EDUCATION

Education was very important in Aztec society. All children were educated until age 14 or 15. Many were educated by their parents at home. Part of their education included memorizing the Aztec "sayings of the old." This is how young people learned the values and traditions of Aztec society.

21

AZTEC CODICES

The Aztecs had a writing system that used **pictographs** and other symbols. They often put their writings into a type of book called a **codex**. The first codices were made by folding up one very long page. Later, pages were attached together. The Aztecs had libraries for storing their handwritten codices. Educated scribes used this writing system to record daily events, the history of the empire, and religious rules.

Many early codices were burned at the start of the Aztec Empire by rulers who wanted to rewrite history to flatter themselves. The Spanish destroyed many more, but about 500 survive from around the time of the Spanish conquest. Often these codices include notes in Spanish or Latin that help researchers understand Aztec language and history.

Boys of the commoner class attended the local telpochcalli, or practical school, where they trained for the military and learned how to build roads and buildings. The sons of nobles attended calmecac, or religious schools, where they were educated in writing, religion, government, and astronomy. Girls were only educated at home.

ARTS AND CULTURE

Poetry and performance were an important part of Aztec culture. Music, plays, and acrobatics were usually part of Aztec festivals. Some Aztec poetry survives today because it was written down during the Spanish conquest using the **Roman alphabet**.

Aztec craftsmen were commoners and held a social position just below merchants. They usually worked for the tlatoani and created carvings and sculpture for religious decoration. Aztecs also made crafts and jewelry from silver, gold, precious gems, and stones such as jade and turquoise. Mosaics were also very common in Aztec art. The Aztecs even made mirrors from **obsidian**, a black reflective stone. They believed their gods watched them through the mirror.

Commoners themselves were not allowed to own works of art—all the great works of art were owned and kept by the upper classes. And the way the people dressed had to reflect their social status. Only the nobility could wear beautiful clothing, headdresses, ceremonial weapons, or jewelry.

ARTISANS MADE BEAUTIFUL OBJECTS FOR NOBLES, USING BRIGHT STONES AND FEATHERS OF BIRDS SUCH AS THE QUETZAL (RIGHT).

Many of the materials used in Aztec art were probably brought into the empire by merchants. There is also evidence that the Aztecs **exported** their own art and **imported** art from other cultures, such as the Mixteca, who lived southwest of the Aztec Empire.

One of the most famous pieces of Aztec art is the great Sun Stone, which is also known as the Calendar Stone. It was found in the ruins of the Templo Mayor in Mexico City. It is disc-shaped and about 12 feet (3.7 m) in diameter—2 feet (61 cm) taller than a basketball net. The stone shows the symbols for the Aztec calendar.

THE GREAT SUN STONE AND A TALL STATUE OF THE GODDESS COATLICUE ARE FAMOUS AZTEC ARTIFACTS ON DISPLAY IN MEXICO CITY.

AZTECS AND MAYANS PLAYED A SIMILAR BALL GAME. IN BOTH, THE STONE RINGS WERE PLACED HIGH ON THE COURT.

SPORTS

The Aztecs played a ball game called tlachtli or ullamaliztli. The sport was played with a solid rubber ball called an ulli that weighed 9 pounds (4 kg). The game was played on a court shaped like a capital letter I with sloping walls up the sides. Players could hit the ball with their hips, knees, and elbows. They had to wear protective clothes because they were often hurt by the stone court—players often ended the game bruised and bleeding. The goal of the game was to pass the ball through the center of a stone ring. Getting the ball through the ring was so difficult that the first team to score a goal won the game. The sport was both entertainment and religious ritual. In fact, most tlachtli courts were built next to temples.

CHAPTER 5

DECLINE AND LEGACY

Moctezuma II was elected huey tlataoni, or emperor, in 1502, at the height of the empire. The empire was large, powerful, and wealthy. But Christopher Columbus had landed across the Gulf of Mexico on the island of Cuba 10 years earlier. Since then, the Spanish had been conquering and taking over the New World, as they called it. In the spring of 1519, the conquistador Hernán Cortés and his expedition landed in Maya territory on the Gulf Coast. A Spanish priest had been shipwrecked there the year before and had learned to speak Maya. With the help of this priest and a slave woman who spoke both Maya and Nahuatl, Cortés was able to form an alliance with the Nahuatl-speaking Tlaxcalteca, traditional enemies of the empire. A combined expedition of Spanish and Tlaxcalteca arrived in Tenochtitlán in 1520. The Spanish were completely in awe of the city on the water and its large army. Moctezuma II welcomed them as honored visitors. But eventually tensions between the Spanish and the Aztecs increased and fighting broke out. Moctezuma II was killed and the Spanish and their Tlaxcalteca allies fled the city.

In the spring of 1521, Cortés returned with a large force of Spanish and natives from many Aztec enemy cities. Cortés laid siege to the city. Even though they were outnumbered, the Spanish and their allies defeated

MOCTEZUMA II RULED THE AZTEC EMPIRE AT ITS PEAK. SEVERAL LEGENDS TELL OF HIS DEATH IN 1520, BUT IT REMAINS UNCLEAR WHO KILLED HIM.

27

DEADLY SMALLPOX

While the Spanish had more powerful weapons, they were outnumbered by great Aztec warriors. But the diseases they brought from Europe turned out to be more deadly than any single weapon. In 1520 there was an outbreak of smallpox, a virus that causes fever and a skin rash called pox. The Spanish had built up immunity over centuries of being exposed to the disease and did not even know they carried it. As many as half the Aztecs died, making it easy for the Spanish to take control of Tenochtitlán. New outbreaks in the 1540s and 1570s helped the Spanish to stay in power, as the Aztec ruling class was destroyed. Some historians believe that 80 percent of the Aztecs died from European diseases within 60 years of the Spaniards' arrival.

the Aztecs in August and destroyed the city of Tenochtitlán. The Spanish founded a new settlement over the ruins which eventually became Mexico City.

At first, the Spanish ruled the empire through **puppet emperors** and treated the pipiltin as noblemen. Many of the conquered cities in the empire were happy to be free of Aztec rule. But soon all the Aztecs were reduced to second-class citizens as Spanish power spread. Many of the indigenous peoples of Mesoamerica were enslaved by the new colonial power.

AZTEC LEGACY

While the Spanish conquest destroyed the Aztec Empire, it did not destroy the Nahua people. The name of the Spanish colony and later the nation of Mexico comes from the Nahua group that led the Aztecs, the Mexica.

Most Mexicans today are descendants of both Aztec and European ancestors. Spanish is the main language spoken in Mexico, but around 1.5 million people in central Mexico still speak the Nahuatl language like their Aztec ancestors.

Mexico City was built over Tenochtitlán. The Templo Mayor was destroyed, and new structures were built over the Aztec city. But many parts of the modern city and country still have their original Aztec names like Tlatelolco and Texcoco. In the twentieth century, the ruins of the temple were discovered, and they were excavated in the 1970s. Archaeologists continue to study the ruins of both Tenochtitlán and Tlatelolco. There are many Aztec archaeological sites throughout the region visited by thousands of Mexicans and foreign tourists every year.

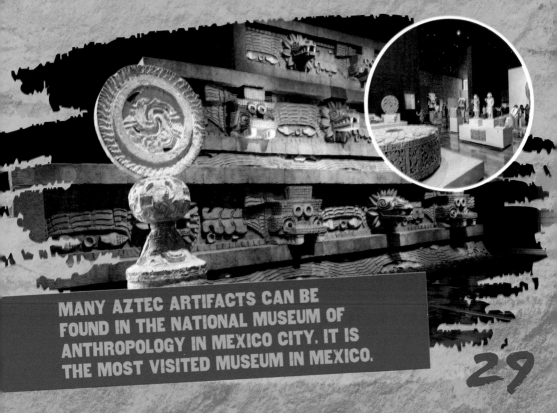

MANY AZTEC ARTIFACTS CAN BE FOUND IN THE NATIONAL MUSEUM OF ANTHROPOLOGY IN MEXICO CITY. IT IS THE MOST VISITED MUSEUM IN MEXICO.

GLOSSARY

adobe: a type of clay usually formed into bricks

alliance: an agreement to work together, usually between organizations or countries

aqueduct: an artificial channel for transporting water

archaeologist: a researcher who studies human history by digging out historical sites and analyzing the remains

codex: an ancient book or handwritten manuscript

conquistadors: the explorers and soldiers sent by Spain to conquer the New World

deities: gods

expedition: a journey taken by a group of people usually for exploration

exported: sold goods to other countries

human sacrifice: the killing of a person in a religious ritual to honor a god

imported: bought goods from other countries

Mesoamerican: term describing the culture and geographical area of Mexico and Central America before the Spanish conquest

mythical: relating to a traditional story or legend, usually involving something supernatural

nomadic: the characteristic of traveling from place to place without a permanent home

obsidian: a hard, glasslike volcanic rock

pictographs: pictures that represent words or ideas

puppet emperor: a local leader who is controlled by an occupying force or foreign government

quarry: to remove stones from the ground

Roman alphabet: the alphabet created for Latin and used for many European languages, such as English and Spanish

shrines: holy places, often including an altar, dedicated to a particular god or person

siege: a military strategy where an army surrounds a town or city, cutting off supplies, and forcing a surrender

umbilical cord: the cord that attaches a baby to the mother in the womb which must be cut once a baby is born

FOR MORE INFORMATION

BOOKS

Burgan, Michael. *Ancient Aztecs*.
New York, NY: Scholastic , 2012.

DK Publishing. *Aztec, Inca & Maya*.
New York, NY: DK Eyewitness Books, 2011.

Raum, Elizabeth. *The Aztec Empire: An Interactive History Adventure*.
North Mankato, MN: Capstone Press, 2012.

WEBSITES

Due to the changing nature of Internet links, PowerKids Press has developed an online list of websites related to the subject of this book. This site is updated regularly. Please use this link to access the list:

www.powerkidslinks.com/aa/aztec

INDEX